20 Easy Knitted Blankets and Throws

From the Staff at Martingale®

Martingale®
Create with Confidence

20 Easy Knitted Blankets and Throws
© 2013 by Martingale & Company®

First published as *The Little Box of Knitted Throws*
© 2005 by Martingale & Company

Martingale®
19021 120th Ave. NE, Ste. 102
Bothell, WA 98011-9511 USA
ShopMartingale.com

Printed in China
18 17 16 15 14   8 7 6 5 4 3 2

Library of Congress Cataloging-in-Publication Data is available upon request.

ISBN: 978-1-60468-305-9

CREDITS

President and CEO • Tom Wierzbicki

Editor in Chief • Mary V. Green

Design Director • Paula Schlosser

Managing Editor • Karen Costello Soltys

Acquisitions Editor: Karen M. Burns

Technical Editor • Ursula Reikes

Cover and Text Designer • Regina Girard

Illustrator • Robin Strobel

Photographer • Brent Kane

MISSION STATEMENT

Dedicated to providing quality products and service to inspire creativity.

ACKNOWLEDGMENTS

We wish to thank the following knitters for their time and talent in making the throws:

Mary V. Green: Garden Gate, Rhythm in Blue, Pretty in Pink

Virginia Lauth: Arbor, Holiday Sampler

Byrle I. McCart: The Men's Club

Jan Moore: Easy Aran Squares, Cabin Cozy

Ursula Reikes: Confetti, Baby Blocks, Sunset Squares, Stained Glass

JoAn Reynolds: Triple Wave, Butterfly Wings

Jan Runkel: Mocha Ripple, Tri-Color Weave

Karen Costello Soltys: School Spirit, Spring Lace

Robin Strobel: Ruby Knights, Diamonds in Denim

Contents

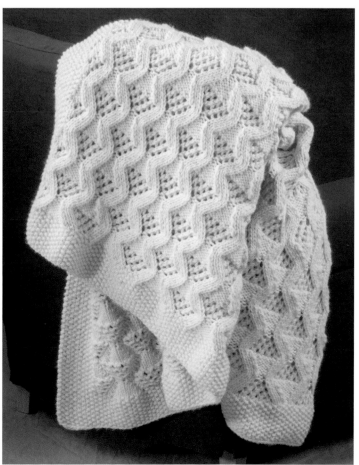

Introduction

Is there anything more comforting or heartwarming than a hand-knitted throw? Regardless of the yarn or pattern used; the size or the color; and whether you call it a throw, an afghan, or a blanket, there's something inherently lovable about a hand-stitched warmer.

This beautiful collection of timeless designs includes soft blankets to tuck around precious little ones, lap throws to chase away the chill, and couch-sized covers big enough to pull up under your chin for a long winter's nap. The stitch patterns are easy to master, ranging from simple garter-stitch squares and stripes to chunky cables and a gorgeous holiday stitch sampler. Soft lacy designs, masculine houndstooth, and colorful teen-perfect patterns round out the collection. These designs are as much fun to knit as they are to use. Some are even reversible, and all make thoughtful gifts.

So go ahead. Knit one for yourself and surround yourself with texture, style, and warmth. Knit one as a gift and bask in the glow of appreciation from the lucky recipient. With all these wonderful patterns to choose from, you'll find lots of reasons to start stitching!

Arbor

The twining pattern and openwork on this beautiful throw are reminiscent of a romantic garden arbor.

APPROXIMATE SIZE

48" x 60"

MATERIALS

10 skeins of Wool-Ease Chunky from Lion Brand Yarn (80% acrylic, 20% wool; 153 yds; 140 g), color 099 Fisherman **5**

Size 10 circular needle (32") or size required to obtain gauge

2 stitch markers

GAUGE

13 sts = 4" in patt

SEED STITCH

(Odd number of sts)

Row 1 (RS): K1, *P1, K1, rep from *.

Row 2: Knit the purl sts and purl the knit sts as they face you.

Rep row 2.

ARBOR PATTERN

(Multiple of 16 sts + 1 st)

Row 1 (RS): K1, *YO, K2, ssk, P7, K2tog, K2, YO, K1, rep from *.

Row 2: P5, *K7, P9, rep from * to last 12 sts, K7, P5.

Row 3: K2, *YO, K2, ssk, P5, K2tog, K2, YO, K2tog, YO, K1, rep from * to last 15 sts, YO, K2, ssk, P5, K2tog, K2, YO, K2.

Row 4: P6, *K5, P11, rep from * to last 11 sts, K5, P6.

Row 5: *K2tog, YO, K1, YO, K2, ssk, P3, K2tog, K2, YO, K2tog, YO, rep from * to last st, K1.

Row 6: P7, *K3, P13, rep from * to last 10 sts, K3, P7.

Row 7: K1, *K2tog, YO, K1, YO, K2, ssk, P1, K2tog, K2, YO, (K2tog, YO) twice, rep from * to last 16 sts, K2tog, YO, K1, YO, K2, ssk, P1, K2tog, K2, YO, K2tog, YO, K2.

Row 8: P8, *K1, P15, rep from * to last 9 sts, K1, P8.

Row 9: P4, *K2tog, K2, YO, K1, YO, K2, ssk, P7, rep from * to last 13 sts, K2tog, K2, YO, K1, YO, K2, ssk, P4.

Row 10: K4, *P9, K7, rep from * to last 13 sts, P9, K4.

Row 11: P3, *K2tog, K2, YO, K2tog, YO, K1, YO, K2, ssk, P5, rep from * to last 14 sts, K2tog, K2, YO, K2tog, YO, K1, YO, K2, ssk, P3.

Row 12: K3, *P11, K5, rep from * to last 14 sts, P11, K3.

Row 13: P2, *K2tog, K2, YO, (K2tog, YO) twice, K1, YO, K2, ssk, P3, rep from * to last 15 sts, K2tog, K2, YO, (K2tog, YO) twice, K1, YO, K2, ssk, P2.

Row 14: K2, *P13, K3, rep from * to last 15 sts, P13, K2.

Row 15: P1, *K2tog, K2, YO, (K2tog, YO) 3 times, K1, YO, K2, ssk, P1, rep from *.

Row 16: K1, *P15, K1, rep from *.

Rep rows 1–16.

DIRECTIONS

CO 149 sts and work 3" in seed st.

Set up patt on next RS row as follows: work 10 sts in seed st, pm, work next 129 sts in arbor patt, pm, work 10 sts in seed st. Cont in established patt, keeping first 10 sts and last 10 sts in seed st until piece measures approx 57", ending with completed row 16 of arbor patt.

Work 3" in seed st. BO all sts in patt.

Weave in ends. Block.

Confetti

Bright, cheerful colors and soft, fuzzy textures combine to make a cuddly throw for Baby.

APPROXIMATE SIZE

36" x 44"

MATERIALS

Main Color (MC): 4 skeins of Encore Worsted from Plymouth Yarn Company (75% acrylic, 25% wool; 200 yds, 100 g) in color 208 (white) [4]

Other Colors: Eskimo DK* from Stylecraft (100% polyester; 98 yds; 50 g) [4] in the following amounts and colors:

1 skein of color 5244 (purple)
1 skein of color 5480 (blue)
1 skein of color 5483 (turquoise)
1 skein of color 5061 (yellow)
1 skein of color 5482 (pink)

Size 9 circular needle (29" long) or size required to obtain gauge

Eskimo DK has been discontinued but may be available from some retailers. Fun Fur Yarn from Lion Brand Yarns is a good substitute, but because Fun Fur has less yardage than Eskimo DK, you'll need 2 skeins of each. Or you'll need approximately 100 yds of equivalent eyelash or novelty yarn in each of the 5 colors.

GAUGE

16 sts = 4" in garter st with MC

GARTER STITCH

Knit every row.

DIRECTIONS

With purple, CO 130 sts and work 7 rows in garter st.

Change to MC and work rem throw in garter st, alternating yarns as follows:

    28 rows of MC
    8 rows of blue
    28 rows of MC
    8 rows of turquoise
    28 rows of MC
    8 rows of yellow
    28 rows of MC
    8 rows of pink
    28 rows of MC
    8 rows of purple
    28 rows of MC
    8 rows of blue
    28 rows of MC
    8 rows of turquoise
    28 rows of MC
    8 rows of yellow
    28 rows of MC
    7 rows of pink

BO sts loosely.

Weave in all ends.

Edging: With RS facing you, use blue to PU 1 st in each garter ridge along one side. Knit 6 rows. BO sts loosely. With RS facing you, use turquoise to PU 1 st in each garter ridge along opposite side. Knit 6 rows. BO sts loosely.

Weave in ends. Block if necessary.

• •

TIP: To keep track of the rows of garter stitch, count the ridges on the right side. One garter ridge equals 2 rows of garter stitch. You should have 14 ridges after working 28 rows of garter stitch. However, because you won't be able to see the garter ridges in the novelty yarn, use a stitch/row counter to keep track of those rows.

• •

Butterfly Wings

*Soft and sweet, this throw is perfect
for a nursery or little girl's room.*

APPROXIMATE SIZE

42" x 48"

MATERIALS

9 skeins of Encore Chunky from Plymouth Yarn Company (75% acrylic, 25% wool; 143 yds; 100 g), color 215 Yellow **5**

Size 10 circular needle (29") or size required to obtain gauge

Size G-6 (4 mm) crochet hook

GAUGE

16 sts = 4" in patt

BUTTERFLY WINGS PATTERN

(Multiple of 26 sts)

Row 1 and every WS row: Purl.

Row 2 (RS): K1, *M1, ssk, K4, K2tog, K3, M1, K2, M1, K3, ssk, K4, K2tog, M1, K2, rep from *, ending last rep with K1 instead of K2.

Row 4: K1, *M1, K1, ssk, K2, K2tog, K4, M1, K2, M1, K4, ssk, K2, K2tog, K1, M1, K2, rep from *, ending last rep with K1 instead of K2.

Row 6: K1, *M1, K2, ssk, K2tog, K5, M1, K2, M1, K5, ssk, K2tog, K2, M1, K2, rep from *, ending last rep with K1 instead of K2.

Row 8: K1, *M1, K3, ssk, K4, K2tog, M1, K2, M1, ssk, K4, K2tog, K3, M1, K2, rep from *, ending last rep with K1 instead of K2.

Row 10: K1, *M1, K4, ssk, K2, K2tog, K1, M1, K2, M1, K1, ssk, K2, K2tog, K4, M1, K2, rep from *, ending last rep with K1 instead of K2.

Row 12: K1, *M1, K5, ssk, K2tog, (K2, M1) twice, K2, ssk, K2tog, K5, M1, K2, rep from *, ending last rep with K1 instead of K2.

Rep rows 1–12.

DIRECTIONS

CO 156 sts and work in butterfly wings patt until piece measures approx 45", ending with completed row 12.

BO sts loosely.

Edging: With crochet hook and RS facing you, work 1 rnd of sc, turn work. Work 1 rnd of sc. See "Crocheted Edges" on page 47.

Weave in ends. Block.

Mocha Ripple

*Soft, cozy yarns in warm neutral tones
are welcome in any decor.*

APPROXIMATE SIZE

48" x 60"

MATERIALS

Pastaza from Cascade Yarns (50% llama, 50% wool;
132 yds; 100 g) 〔5〕 in the following amounts and colors:

6 skeins of color 080 Cinnamon Heather
6 skeins of color 004 Camel

Size 13 circular needle (32") or size required to
obtain gauge

GAUGE

12 sts = 4" in patt

GARTER-STITCH CHEVRON PATTERN

(Multiple of 11 sts)

Rows 1–5: With cinnamon, knit.

Row 6 (RS): Change to camel, *K2tog, K2, K1f&b twice, K3, ssk, rep from *.

Row 7: Purl.

Rows 8–11: Rep rows 6 and 7 twice.

Row 12: Change to cinnamon, rep row 6.

Rep rows 1–12.

DIRECTIONS

With cinnamon, CO 143 sts loosely.

Beg garter-stitch chevron patt and work until piece measures approx 60", ending with completed row 5. Cut the yarn when you change from one color to the other and weave in ends later.

BO sts loosely.

Weave in ends. Block.

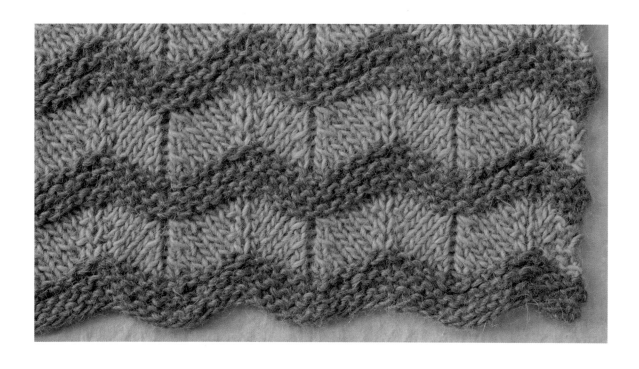

Garden Gate

Gorgeous texture and soft, chunky wool make this the perfect throw to snuggle under on the coldest winter days.

APPROXIMATE SIZE
39" x 56"

MATERIALS
7 skeins of Magnum from Cascade Yarns (100% wool; 123 yds; 250 g), color 9338 Moss (6)

Size 13 circular needle (29" or longer) or size required to obtain gauge

GAUGE
8 sts = 4" in patt

GATEPOST PATTERN
(Multiple of 12 sts + 6 sts)

Row 1 (RS): K2, P1, *P1, K2, P6, K2, P1, rep from * to last 3 sts, P1, K2.

Row 2 and all WS rows: Knit the knit sts and purl the purl sts as they face you.

Row 3: K2, P1, *P1, K10, P1, rep from * to last 3 sts, P1, K2.

Row 5: K3, *K5, P2, K5, rep from * to last 3 sts, K3.

Row 7: P3, *P3, K2, P2, K2, P3, rep from * to last 3 sts, P3.

Row 9: Rep row 5.

Row 11: Rep row 3.

Row 12: Knit the knit sts and purl the purl sts as they face you.

Rep rows 1–12.

DIRECTIONS
CO 78 sts. Work in gatepost patt until piece measures approx 56", ending with completed row 12.

BO sts loosely.

Weave in ends. Block.

School Spirit

**Stitch this in your favorite school's colors
for a perfect addition to a dorm room or den.**

APPROXIMATE SIZE

50" x 60"

MATERIALS

128 Tweed* from Cascade Yarns (100% wool; 128 yds; 100 g) (**5**) in the following amounts and colors:

7 skeins of color 621 Dark Plum
7 skeins of color 616 Silver

Size 9 circular needle (48" long) or size required to obtain gauge

Size G-6 (4 mm) crochet hook

128 Tweed has been discontinued, but 128 Superwash and 128 Chunky are available. Or substitute 900 yds of each color of an equivalent bulky-weight yarn.

GAUGE

16 sts = 4" in patt

DIAGONAL SLIP-STITCH PATTERN

(Multiple of 3 sts + 2 sts)

Row 1 (RS): With plum, K3, sl 1 wyib, *K2, sl 1 wyib, rep from * to last st, K1.

Row 2 and all WS rows: Purl across, slipping sts of previous row wyif.

Row 3: With silver, K1, *sl 1 wyib, K2, rep from * to last st, K1.

Row 5: With plum, K2, *sl 1 wyib, K2, rep from * to end.

Row 7: With silver, K3, sl 1 wyib, *K2, sl 1 wyib, rep from * to last st, K1.

Row 9: With plum, K1, *sl 1 wyib, K2, rep from * to last st, K1.

Row 11: With silver, K2, *sl 1 wyib, K2, rep from * to end.

Row 12: Purl across, slipping sts of previous row wyif.

Rep rows 1–12.

DIRECTIONS

With plum, CO 194 sts and purl 1 row (WS).

Beg diagonal slip-stitch patt and work in patt until throw measures approx 58", ending with silver purl row. Knit 1 row in plum, then BO .

Edging: With crochet hook and RS facing you, work 3 rnds of sc in the following color sequence: 1 rnd of plum, 1 rnd of silver, 1 rnd of plum. See "Crocheted Edges" on page 47.

Weave in ends. Block.

Triple Wave

The classic chevron pattern makes a comeback in updated colors and chunky yarn.

APPROXIMATE SIZE

54" x 64"

MATERIALS

Wool-Ease Thick & Quick from Lion Brand Yarn (86% acrylic, 10% wool, 4% rayon; 108 yds; 170 g) **6** in the following amounts and colors:

4 skeins of color 149 Charcoal
4 skeins of color 402 Wheat
4 skeins of color 130 Green

Size 13 circular needle (32") or size required to obtain gauge

GAUGE

11 sts = 4" in patt

CHEVRON PATTERN

(Multiple of 12 sts + 3 sts)

Row 1 (RS): K1, ssk, *K4, YO, K1, YO, K4, s2Kp; rep from * to last 12 sts, K4, YO, K1, YO, K4, K2tog, K1.

Row 2: Purl.

Rep rows 1 and 2.

COLOR SEQUENCE

12 rows of charcoal
12 rows of green
12 rows of wheat

DIRECTIONS

With charcoal, CO 147 sts and beg chevron patt. Cont in patt and work 36-row color sequence a total of 4 times.

BO sts loosely.

Weave in ends. Block.

Double-Ridged Rib

Double Moss

Diamond Brocade

Basket Rib

Holiday Sampler

Show off your stitching skills with this texture-filled sampler.

APPROXIMATE SIZE

48" x 58"

MATERIALS

Encore Chunky from Plymouth Yarn Company (75% acrylic, 25% wool; 143 yds; 100 g) **⑤** in the following amounts and colors:

MC   8 skeins of color 146 (off-white)
CC1   4 skeins of color 204 (green)
CC2   2 skeins of color 9601 (red)

Size 10 circular needle (32") or size required to obtain gauge

GAUGE

14 sts = 4" in St st

SEED STITCH

Row 1 (RS): K1, *P1, K1, rep from *.

Row 2: Knit the purl sts and purl the knit sts as they face you.

Rep row 2.

DOUBLE-RIDGED RIB PATTERN

Rows 1 (RS), 2, 5, 6: Knit.

Rows 3, 8: P1, *K1, P1, rep from *.

Rows 4, 7: K1, *P1, K1, rep from *.

Rep rows 1–8.

DOUBLE MOSS PATTERN

Rows 1(RS), 4: K1, *P1, K1, rep from *.

Rows 2, 3: P1, *K1, P1, rep from *.

Rep rows 1–4.

DIAMOND BROCADE PATTERN

Row 1 (RS): K4, *P1, K7, rep from * to last 5 sts, P1, K4.

Rows 2, 8: P3, *K1, P1, K1, P5, rep from * to last 6 sts, K1, P1, K1, P3.

Rows 3, 7: K2, *P1, K3, rep from * to last 3 sts, P1, K2.

Rows 4, 6: P1, *K1, P5, K1, P1, rep from *.

Row 5: *P1, K7, rep from * to last st, P1.

Rep rows 1–8.

BASKET RIB PATTERN

Row 1 (RS): Knit.

Row 2: Purl.

Row 3: K1, *sl 1 wyib, K1, rep from *.

Row 4: K1, *sl 1 wyif, K1, rep from *.

Rep rows 1–4.

STRIPE A

6 rows CC1, 4 rows CC2, 6 rows CC1

STRIPE B

6 rows CC2, 4 rows CC1, 6 rows CC2

DIRECTIONS

With CC1, CO 153 sts and work stripe A once in seed st.

With MC, work double-ridged rib patt for 10", end with WS row. Knit 2 rows.

Work stripe B once in St st.

With MC, knit 2 rows. Work double moss patt for 10", end with WS row. Knit 2 rows.

Work stripe A once in St st.

With MC, knit 2 rows. Work diamond brocade patt for 10", end with WS row. Knit 2 rows.

Work stripe B once in St st.

With MC, knit 2 rows. Work basket rib patt for 10", end with WS row. Knit 2 rows.

Work stripe A once as follows: knit first row, beg seed st on next row, and work in seed st for remainder of stripe. BO all sts.

Edging: With CC1, PU sts in every other row along one side (approx 165 sts) and work stripe A once in seed st. BO sts loosely. Rep edging on opposite side.

Weave in ends. Block.

Ruby Knights

*Alternating knit and purl squares work up
quickly into a rich chessboard pattern.*

APPROXIMATE SIZE

50" x 56"

MATERIALS

10 skeins of Wool-Ease Thick & Quick from Lion Brand
Yarn (86% acrylic, 10% wool, 4% rayon; 108 yds;
170 g), color 138 Cranberry **⑥**

Size 15 circular needle (32") or size required to
obtain gauge

Size L-11 (8 mm) crochet hook

GAUGE

9 sts = 4" in patt

CHESSBOARD PATTERN

(Multiple of 12 sts + 1 st)

Rows 1, 3, 5: *K7, P5, rep from * to last st, K1.

Row 2 and all even-numbered rows: Knit the knit sts
and purl the purl sts as they face you.

Rows 7, 9, 11: K1, *P5, K7, rep from *.

Row 12: Rep row 2.

Rep rows 1–12.

DIRECTIONS

CO 109 sts. Beg chessboard patt and work rows 1–12 a
total of 16 times.

BO sts loosely in patt.

Edging: With crochet hook and RS facing you, work 2
rnds of sc. See "Crocheted Edges" on page 47.

Weave in ends. Block.

Tri-Color Weave

This interesting pattern is reminiscent of a woven blanket, but much easier to create!

APPROXIMATE SIZE

46" x 62"

MATERIALS

Encore Chunky from Plymouth Yarn Company (75% acrylic, 25% wool; 143 yds; 100 g) **5** in the following amounts and colors:

4 skeins of color 848 (navy)
8 skeins of color 146 (off-white)
4 skeins of color 9601 (red)

Size 11 circular needle (32") or size required to obtain gauge

GAUGE

13½ sts = 4" in patt

GARTER STITCH

Knit every row.

RIBBED TWEED STITCH

(Multiple of 6 sts + 13 sts)

Row 1: K6, *sl 1 wyib, K5, rep from * to last 7 sts, sl 1 wyib, K6.

Row 2: Knit across, sl the sl sts of previous row wyif.

Row 3: K9, *sl 1 wyib, K5, rep from * to last 10 sts, sl 1 wyib, K9.

Row 4: Knit across, sl the sl sts of previous row wyif.

Rep rows 1–4 a total of 5 times (for a total of 20 rows) for each color sequence.

DIRECTIONS

With navy, CO 157 sts and work garter-st border with 2 rows of each color in the following sequence:

Navy
Off-white
Red
Off-white
Navy
Off-white

Change to red and work ribbed tweed st as follows:

Rows 1 and 2 in red
Rows 3 and 4 in off-white

Rep rows 1–4 of ribbed tweed st in this color sequence for a total of 20 rows.

Work ribbed tweed st in 20-row color sequence as follows:

Rows 1 and 2 in navy
Rows 3 and 4 in off-white

Rep alternating red and blue 20-row color sequences until you've worked a total of 9 red/off-white and 9 blue/off-white sequences, ending with a blue/off-white sequence. Work 1 more color sequence in red/off-white, ending with completed row 18 in red.

Work garter-st border with 2 rows of each color in the following sequence:

Off-white
Navy
Off-white
Red
Off-white
Navy

BO sts loosely.

Weave in ends. Block.

Easy Aran Squares

*Classic cables are stitched a block at a time,
making this an ideal take-along project.*

APPROXIMATE SIZE

50" x 68"

MATERIALS

18 skeins of Encore Chunky from Plymouth Yarn (75% acrylic, 25% wool; 143 yds; 100 g), color 240 (tan) 🧶**5**

Size 11 circular needles (24") or size required to obtain gauge

Cable needle

Size K-10½ (6.5 mm) crochet hook

GAUGE

11 sts = 4" in patt

SQUARE

C4B: Sl 2 sts to cn and hold at back of work, K2, K2 from cn.

C8B: Sl 4 sts to cn and hold at back of work, K4, K4 from cn.

Note: Rows 4 and 8 are *not* the same; there is no twist in the large cable on row 8.

CO 44 sts and work patt as follows:

Row 1 (WS): (K3, P2, K3, P4) 3 times, K3, P2, K3.

Row 2 (RS) (Inc row): *P3, M1, K2, M1, P3, (M1, K1) twice, (K1, M1) twice, rep from * 2 more times, P3, M1, K2, M1, P3—64 sts.

Row 3 and all other WS rows: (K3, P4, K3, P8) 3 times, K3, P4, K3.

Row 4: (P3, C4B, P3, C8B) 3 times, P3, C4B, P3.

Row 6: (P3, K4, P3, K8) 3 times, P3, K4, P3.

Row 8: (P3, C4B, P3, K8) 3 times, P3, C4B, P3.

Row 10: Rep row 6.

Rep rows 3–10 until 70 total rows have been completed, ending with row 6.

Row 71 (Dec row): *K3, (P2tog) twice, K3, (P2tog) 4 times, rep from * 2 more times, K3, (P2tog) twice, K3—44 sts.

Next row: BO in patt; do not fasten off. Place last st from BO on crochet hook, ch 1, work 1 rnd sc all around square, working 41 sc on each side and 3 sc in each corner. Fasten off.

DIRECTIONS

Make 12 squares.

Alternating directions of cables, join squares into 3 rows of 4 squares each. Refer to "Joining Squares" on page 47 for detailed instructions. Join rows in same manner.

Edging: With crochet hook and RS facing you, work 1 rnd of hdc, do not turn work. Ch 1, work 1 rnd of sc, working in third loop behind and below back loop of previous row, turn work. With WS facing you, ch 2, work 1 rnd of hdc. See "Crocheted Edges" on page 47.

Weave in ends. Block.

The Men's Club

In rich shades of charcoal and cranberry, this houndstooth throw will look great draped over his favorite chair.

APPROXIMATE SIZE

48" x 60"

MATERIALS

Wool-Ease Thick & Quick from Lion Brand Yarn (80% acrylic, 20% wool; 108 yds; 170 g) (6) in the following amounts and colors:

6 skeins of color 138 Cranberry

6 skeins of color 149 Charcoal

Size 13 circular needle (29") or size required to obtain gauge

2 stitch markers

GAUGE

9 sts = 4" in patt

GARTER STITCH

Knit every row.

HOUNDSTOOTH PATTERN

(Multiple of 3 sts)

Row 1 (RS): With cranberry, K1, *sl 1 wyib, K2, rep from * to last 2 sts, sl 1 wyib, K1.

Row 2: Purl.

Row 3: With charcoal, *sl 1 wyib, K2, rep from * to end.

Row 4: Purl.

Rep rows 1–4.

DIRECTIONS

With charcoal, CO 108 sts and work bottom border in garter st as follows. Carry yarns along edge, placing old yarn on top of new yarn and toward the left.

> 2 rows of charcoal
> 2 rows of cranberry
> 2 rows of charcoal
> 2 rows of cranberry
> 2 rows of charcoal

Set up patt on next RS row as follows: Work first 6 sts in garter st, pm, work next 96 sts in houndstooth patt, pm, work last 6 sts in garter st. Work in established patt until piece is approx 57½" from beg, ending with completed row 2.

Work top border as for bottom border. BO sts loosely in charcoal.

Weave in ends. Block.

Cabin Cozy

Bring a rustic touch to any room with this inviting throw.
The slip-stitch rows add a unique accent.

APPROXIMATE SIZE

48" x 72"

MATERIALS

Lamb's Pride Bulky from Brown Sheep Company (85% wool, 15% mohair; 125 yds; 113 g) **5** in the following amounts and colors:

6 skeins of color M-02 Brown Heather
3 skeins of color M-82 Blue Flannel
3 skeins of color M-68 Pine Tree
3 skeins of color M-181 Prairie Fire

Size 10½ circular needle (32") or size required to obtain gauge

2 stitch markers

GAUGE

12 sts = 4" in patt

ABBREVIATIONS

Sl 2 wyif: Move yarn to front of work and sl 2 sts purlwise.

Sl 2 wyib: Move yarn to back of work and sl 2 sts purlwise.

DIRECTIONS

With brown, CO 146 sts and knit 13 rows.

Work body of throw as follows:

Row 1 (RS): With blue, K8, pm, K130, pm, K8.

Row 2: With blue, K8, P130, K8.

Row 3: With brown, K8, (sl 2 wyif, K2) across to last 10 sts, sl 2 wyif, K8.

Row 4: With brown, K8, P2, (sl 2 wyib, P2) across to last 8 sts, K8.

Rows 5–12: Rep rows 1–4.

Row 13: With blue, knit.

Row 14: With blue, K8, P130, K8.

Rows 15–36: Rep rows 13 and 14.

Rows 37–46: Rep rows 3–12.

Rows 47–58: With brown, rep rows 13 and 14.

Rows 59–116: Rep rows 1–58, substituting pine for blue.

Rows 117–174: Rep rows 1–58, substituting prairie for blue.

Rows 175–232: Rep rows 1–58 with blue.

Rows 233–290: Rep rows 59–116.

Rows 291–336: Rep rows 1–46, substituting prairie for blue.

With brown, knit 13 rows.

BO sts knitwise.

Weave in ends. Block.

Diamonds in Denim

Bulky yarn worked in an easy knit-and-purl pattern creates a lapful of texture.

APPROXIMATE SIZE

44" x 54"

MATERIALS

15 skeins of Blizzard* from Reynolds (65% alpaca, 35% acrylic; 66 yds; 100 g), color 683 Indigo 6

Size 15 circular needle (32") or size required to obtain gauge

2 stitch markers

This yarn has been discontinued. Substitute 990 yds of an equivalent super-bulky weight yarn.

GAUGE

9 sts = 4" in patt

SEED STITCH

Row 1 (RS): K1, *P1, K1, rep from *.

Row 2: Knit the purl sts and purl the knit sts as they face you.

Rep row 2.

KNIT AND PURL DIAMOND PATTERN

(Multiple of 10 sts + 1 st)

Row 1 (RS): *K5, P1, K4, rep from * to last st, K1.

Row 2 and all WS rows: Knit the knit sts and purl the purl sts as they face you.

Row 3: *K4, P3, K3, rep from * to last st, K1.

Row 5: *K3, P5, K2, rep from * to last st, K1.

Row 7: *K2, P7, K1, rep from * to last st, K1.

Row 9: *K1, P9, rep from * to last st, K1.

Row 11: Rep row 7.

Row 13: Rep row 5.

Row 15: Rep row 3.

Row 16: Rep row 2.

Rep rows 1–16.

DIRECTIONS

CO 99 sts and work 6 rows in seed st.

Set up patt on next RS row as follows: Work first 4 sts in seed st, pm, work next 91 sts in knit and purl diamond patt, pm, work last 4 sts in seed st. Cont in established patt, working first 4 and last 4 sts in seed st until throw measures approx 51½", ending with completed row 16 of knit and purl diamond patt. Work rows 1 and 2 of knit and purl diamond patt once more.

Work 6 rows in seed st.

BO sts loosely in patt.

Weave in ends. Block.

Sunset Squares

**This gorgeous mitered-squares throw glows
with the colors of the evening sky.**

APPROXIMATE SIZE

42" x 50"

MATERIALS

16 skeins of Kureyon from Noro (100% wool; 110 yds;
50 g), color 102 (**4**)

Size 8 needles or size required to obtain gauge

Tapestry needle

Size G-6 (4 mm) crochet hook

GAUGE

16 sts = 4" in patt after blocking

MITERED SQUARE

(8" x 8")

Slip first stitch of each right side row with the yarn in
back. Slip last stitch of each right side row with the yarn
in front, except for the right side rows just before a purl
row, where you will slip the last stitch with the yarn in
back. The first and last slipped stitches create a nice edge
for joining squares through the back loops.

CO 61 sts.

Row 1 (RS): Sl 1 wyib, K28, s2Kp, K28, sl 1 wyif.

**Rows 2, 6, 8, 12, 14, 18, 20, 24, 26, 30, 32, 36, 38,
42, 44, 48, 50, 52, 54, 56:** Knit.

Row 3: Sl 1 wyib, K27, s2Kp, K27, sl 1 wyib.

Rows 4, 10, 16, 22, 28, 34, 40, 46: Purl.

Row 5: Sl 1 wyib, K26, s2Kp, K26, sl 1 wyif.

Row 7: Sl 1 wyib, K25, s2Kp, K25, sl 1 wyif.

Row 9: Sl 1 wyib, K24, s2Kp, K24, sl 1 wyib.

Row 11: Sl 1 wyib, K23, s2Kp, K23, sl 1 wyif.

Cont RS rows in this manner, working 1 less st before
and after the s2Kp until 3 sts rem (row 57).

Row 58: Knit.

Row 59: S2Kp. Fasten off.

DIRECTIONS

Make 30 squares; you will get 2 squares from
each skein.

Arrange squares in 5 rows of 6 squares each. Sew
squares tog in rows using a tapestry needle and an overcast st (page 47). Join rows in the same manner.

Edging: With crochet hook and RS facing you, work
1 rnd of sc. Work 1 rnd of sc in back loop only. See
"Crocheted Edges" on page 47.

Weave in ends. Block.

Rhythm in Blue

The undulating flame pattern of this throw really shines when stitched in a single bold color.

APPROXIMATE SIZE

48" x 60"

MATERIALS

12 skeins of Pastaza from Cascade Yarns (50% llama, 50% wool; 132 yds; 100 g), color 1019 (royal blue) 🌀5

Size 10 circular needle (29") or size required to obtain gauge

GAUGE

15 sts = 4" in patt

SEED STITCH

Row 1 (RS): *K1, P1, rep from *.

Row 2: Knit the purl sts and purl the knit sts as they face you.

Rep row 2.

FLAME WAVE PATTERN

(Multiple of 7 sts + 5 sts)

Row 1 and all WS rows: Purl.

Row 2 (RS): K4, *ssk, K5, M1, rep from * to last st, K1.

Row 4: K4, *ssk, K4, M1, K1, rep from * to last st, K1.

Row 6: K4, *ssk, K3, M1, K2, rep from * to last st, K1.

Row 8: K4, *ssk, K2, M1, K3, rep from * to last st, K1.

Row 10: K4, *ssk, K1, M1, K4, rep from * to last st, K1.

Row 12: K4, *ssk, M1, K5, rep from * to last st, K1.

Row 14: K1, *M1, K5, K2tog, rep from * to last 4 sts, K4.

Row 16: K1, *K1, M1, K4, K2tog, rep from * to last 4 sts, K4.

Row 18: K1, *K2, M1, K3, K2tog, rep from * to last 4 sts, K4.

Row 20: K1, *K3, M1, K2, K2tog, rep from * to last 4 sts, K4.

Row 22: K1, *K4, M1, K1, K2tog, rep from * to last 4 sts, K4.

Row 24: K1, *K5, M1, K2tog, rep from * to last 4 sts, K4.

DIRECTIONS

CO 180 sts and work in seed st for 11 rows.

On next RS row, beg flame wave patt and work in patt until throw measures approx 58", ending with completed row 12 or 24.

Work 11 rows in seed st.

BO sts loosely in patt.

Weave in ends. Block gently.

Baby Blocks

Quick-to-stitch blocks are made one at a time and then sewn together in this pretty baby throw.

APPROXIMATE SIZE

35" x 43"

MATERIALS

Encore Worsted from Plymouth Yarn Company (75% wool, 25% acrylic; 200 yds; 100 g) **4** in the following amounts and colors:

2 skeins of color 793 (blue)
2 skeins of color 896 (yellow)
2 skeins of color 029 (pink)
2 skeins of color 1201 (aqua)

Size 8 needles or size required to obtain gauge

Size G-6 (4 mm) crochet hook

Tapestry needle

GAUGE

17 sts = 4" in seed st and garter st

SEED STITCH

Row 1: *K1, P1, rep from *.

Row 2: Knit the purl sts and purl the knit sts as they face you.

Rep row 2.

GARTER STITCH

Knit every row.

DIRECTIONS

Make 1 square (7½" x 7½") as follows:

With blue, CO 32 sts, and work 18 rows in seed st.

Switch to yellow and work 20 rows in garter st.

Switch to blue and knit 1 row, work 17 rows in seed st. BO in patt on next row.

With aqua and crochet hook, work 1 row sc all around square, working 3 sc in each corner. Work 1 more row of sc all around square, working into back loops only and working 3 sc in each corner. Fasten off and weave in ends.

Working the garter-st section in yellow on all squares, make 10 squares each in the following color combinations for a total of 20 squares:

Blue seed st, yellow garter st, blue seed st

Pink seed st, yellow garter st, pink seed st

FINISHING

Arrange squares in 4 rows of 5 squares each. With aqua and tapestry needle, sew squares tog using an overcast st (page 47). Join rows in same manner.

Edging: With crochet hook, RS facing you, and aqua, work 1 rnd of dc in back loop only. Work 1 rnd of sc in back loop only. See "Crocheted Edges" on page 47.

Weave in ends. Block.

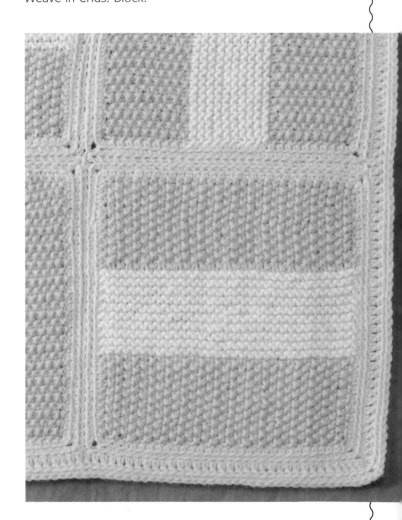

Spring Lace

Light as a feather and soft as a spring breeze, this fabulous throw practically guarantees sweet dreams.

APPROXIMATE SIZE

48" x 60"

MATERIALS

12 skeins of Baby Alpaca Brush from Plymouth Yarn Company (80% baby alpaca, 20% acrylic; 110 yds, 50 g), color 1477 (celery green) **⑤**

Size 9 circular needle (40") or size required to obtain gauge

GAUGE

13 sts = 4" in patt

LACY ZIGZAG PATTERN

(Multiple of 6 sts + 1 st)

Rows 1, 3, 5 (RS): *Ssk, K2, YO, K2, rep from * to last st, K1.

Row 2 and all WS rows: Purl.

Rows 7, 9, 11: K3, *YO, K2, K2tog, K2, rep from * to last 4 sts, YO, K2, K2tog.

Row 12: Purl.

Rep rows 1–12.

DIRECTIONS

CO 157 sts and work bottom border as follows:

Knit 1 row (WS).
Purl 1 row.
Knit 2 rows.
Purl 1 row.

Beg lacy zigzag patt on next RS row and work until piece measures approx 59", ending with completed row 12.

Work top border as follows:

Knit 2 rows.
Purl 1 row.
Knit 1 row.

BO sts loosely.

Weave in ends. Block gently.

Pretty in Pink

. . . or in any other color! This easy pattern stitches up quickly for a great room accent.

APPROXIMATE SIZE

48" x 56"

MATERIALS

11 skeins of 128 from Cascade Yarns (100% wool; 128 yds; 100 g), color 7802 Cerise (**5**)

Size 10 circular needle (29") or size required to obtain gauge

2 ring markers

GAUGE

13 sts = 4" in patt

GARTER STITCH

Knit every row.

WIDE DIAGONAL-RIB PATTERN

(Multiple of 8 sts)

Row 1 (RS): *P6, K2, rep from *.

Row 2 and all WS rows: Knit the knit sts and purl the purl sts as they face you.

Row 3: P5, K2, *P6, K2, rep from * to last st, P1.

Row 5: P4, K2, *P6, K2, rep from * to last 2 sts, P2.

Row 7: P3, K2, *P6, K2, rep from * to last 3 sts, P3.

Row 9: P2, K2, *P6, K2, rep from * to last 4 sts, P4.

Row 11: P1, K2, *P6, K2, rep from * to last 5 sts, P5.

Row 13: K2, *P6, K2, rep from * to last 6 sts, P6.

Row 15: K1, *P6, K2, rep from * to last 7 sts, P6, K1.

Row 16: Rep row 2.

Rep rows 1–16.

DIRECTIONS

CO 158 sts and work 2 rows in garter st, then work in St st until piece measures 2", ending with completed WS row.

Set up patt st on next RS row as follows: K7, pm, work next 144 sts in wide diagonal-rib patt, pm, K7. Cont in established patt, keeping first 7 sts and last 7 sts in St st until piece measures approx 54", ending with row 16.

Work in St st for 1¾", then work 2 rows of garter st. BO sts loosely.

Weave in ends. Block.

Stained Glass

Easy garter-stitch squares and rectangles are joined with simple crochet in this colorful throw.

APPROXIMATE SIZE

40" x 52"

MATERIALS

Canadiana from Patons (100% acrylic; 205 yds; 100 g) **4** in the following amounts and colors:

1 skein of color 10615 Cherished Yellow
1 skein of color 10344 Medium Amethyst
1 skein of color 10420 Cherished Pink
1 skein of color 10743 Pale Teal
1 skein of color 10725 Clearwater Blue
1 skein of color 10110 Navy

Size 8 needles or size required to obtain gauge

Size G-6 (4 mm) crochet hook

Tapestry needle

GAUGE

16 sts = 4" in garter st

GARTER STITCH

Knit every row.

DIRECTIONS

Small rectangle (4" x 6"): CO 24 sts, work 30 rows in garter st. BO loosely.

Square (6" x 6"): CO 24 sts, work 46 rows in garter st. BO loosely.

Large rectangle (6" x 8"): CO 24 sts, work 62 rows in garter st. BO loosely.

From **each** of the yellow, amethyst, pink, teal, and blue yarns, make 2 small rectangles, 2 squares, and 2 large rectangles, for a total of 30 pieces.

With crochet hook and navy, work 1 rnd of sc all around each piece, working 3 sc in each corner, join with sl st into first sc. Work 1 more rnd of sc all around, working into back loops only, join and fasten off.

Arrange pieces into 5 rows, mixing colors as desired, so that there are 2 small rectangles, 2 squares, and 2 large rectangles in each row. With tapestry needle and navy, sew squares tog in rows using an overcast st (page 47). Join rows in same manner.

Edging: With crochet hook, RS facing you, and navy, work 1 rnd of sc, work 3 rnds of dc in back loop only, then work 1 rnd of sc in back loop only. See "Crocheted Edges" on page 47.

Weave in ends. Block.

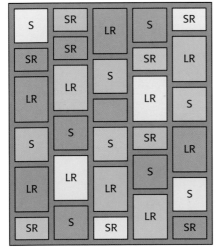

SR = small rectangle
S = square
LR = large rectangle

Abbreviations and Glossary

approx	approximately	**pm**	place marker
beg	begin(ning)	**PU**	pick up and knit
BO	bind off	**RS**	right side
ch	chain	**rem**	remain(ing)
cn	cable needle	**rep**	repeat(ing)
CO	cast on	**rnd(s)**	round(s)
cont	continue	**s2Kp**	slip 2 stitches together as if to knit, knit 1 stitch, pass the 2 slipped stitches over the knit stitch—2 stitches decreased
dc	double crochet		
dec	decrease		
g	grams	**sc**	single crochet
hdc	half double crochet	**sl**	slip
inc	increase	**ssk**	Slip one stitch as if to knit, then slip a second stitch as if to knit. Insert the left needle from left to right into the front of both slipped stitches and knit them together—1 stitch decreased
K	knit		
K1f&b	knit 1 stitch through front loop and 1 stitch through back loop of same stitch—1 stitch increased		
		st(s)	stitch(es)
K2tog	knit 2 stitches together—1 stitch decreased	**St st**	stockinette stitch: knit on RS rows, purl on WS rows
M1	make 1 stitch: make new stitch by lifting horizontal bar between 2 stitches from front to back with left needle and knitting into back of loop—1 stitch increased	**tog**	together
		WS	wrong side
		wyib	with yarn in back
mm	millimeter	**wyif**	with yarn in front
P	purl	**yds**	yards
P2tog	purl 2 stitches together—1 stitch decreased	**YO**	yarn over
patt	pattern		

Helpful Information

JOINING SQUARES

Use these instructions to join the squares in Easy Aran Squares on page 27.

To join squares, place 2 squares side by side with right sides facing up and cables at right angles to each other. With slip knot on crochet hook and working yarn underneath and between the 2 squares, *insert hook from right side through both loops at edge on first square, yarn over and pull through stitch (2 loops on hook), insert hook from right side through both loops of corresponding stitch on second square, yarn over and pull through stitch (3 loops on hook), yarn over and pull through all 3 loops, repeating from * to end. Remember to keep the working yarn underneath and between the squares.

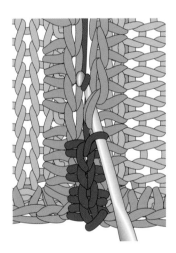

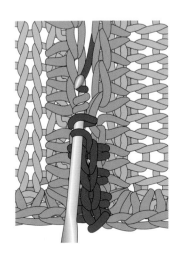

OVERCAST STITCH

Place squares next to each other with right sides facing up. With tapestry needle and strand of yarn, insert needle from back to front in back loop of first edge stitch at corner of first square, leaving a 3" tail, then insert needle from back to front into back loop of corresponding corner stitch on second square. *Insert needle from front to back into back loop of next stitch on first square, then insert needle from back to front of next stitch on second square; draw yarn through but don't pull too tight.* A short diagonal line will appear between the back loops of the 2 squares. Repeat from * to * to end of squares; fasten off and weave in ends.

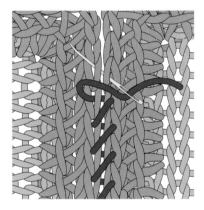

CROCHETED EDGES

Several of the throws call for 2 or more rounds of crochet around the entire edge. Because crochet stitches are denser than knit stitches, the edges of the throw can become rippled if the crochet stitches are not worked evenly along the edges. When working the first row of crochet, start by working 1 crochet stitch in each stitch or end of row. If the edge appears to be rippling, try crocheting in 2 out of every 3 stitches or rows, or 3 out of every 4 stitches or rows. Consider a different size crochet hook if you have trouble achieving the correct tension.

Work 3 stitches (in same stitch as the round) in each corner stitch. Join the rounds with a slip stitch in the beginning stitch. Fasten off at the end of the last round. Do not turn the work unless directed to do so. On subsequent rounds, work 1 stitch in each stitch from the previous row, except for the corners, where you will work 3 stitches. Work into both loops of the stitches from the previous round unless otherwise instructed.

STANDARD YARN-WEIGHT SYSTEM

Yarn Weight Symbol and Category Names	**1** SUPER FINE	**2** FINE	**3** LIGHT	**4** MEDIUM	**5** BULKY	**6** SUPER BULKY
Types of Yarns in Category	Sock, Fingering, Baby	Sport, Baby	DK, Light Worsted	Worsted, Afghan, Aran	Chunky, Craft, Rug	Bulky, Roving
Knit Gauge Range* in Stockinette Stitch to 4"	27 to 32 sts	23 to 26 sts	21 to 24 sts	16 to 20 sts	12 to 15 sts	6 to 11 sts
Recommended Needle in Metric Size Range	2.25 to 3.25 mm	3.25 to 3.75 mm	3.75 to 4.5 mm	4.5 to 5.5 mm	5.5 to 8 mm	8 mm and larger
Recommended Needle in US Size Range	1 to 3	3 to 5	5 to 7	7 to 9	9 to 11	11 and larger

*These are guidelines only. The above reflect the most commonly used gauges and needle or hook sizes for specific yarn categories.

METRIC CONVERSION

Use these handy formulas for easy conversions.

Yards x 0.9144 = meters

Meters x 1.0936 = yards

Grams x 0.0352 = ounces

Ounces x 28.35 = grams